Mini Artist

Painting

Paul Calver

WINDMILL
BOOKS™
New York

Published in 2015 by Windmill Books, An Imprint of Rosen Publishing
29 East 21st Street, New York, NY 10010

Editor for Windmill: Joshua Shadowens

Photo Credits: Illustrations by Fiona Gowen; Images on pages 2 and 3 © fotolia.com.

Library of Congress Cataloging-in-Publication Data

Calver, Paul.
 Painting / by Paul Calver.
    pages cm. — (Mini artist)
 Includes index.
 ISBN 978-1-4777-9119-6 (library binding) — ISBN 978-1-4777-9120-2 (pbk.) —
ISBN 978-1-4777-9121-9 (6-pack)
 1. Painting—Technique—Juvenile literature. I. Title.
 ND1146.C345 2015
 751.4—dc23
                                    2014001200

Manufactured in the United States of America

CPSIA Compliance Information: Batch #WS14WM: For Further Information contact Windmill Books, New York, New York at 1-866-478-0556

Mini Artist **Painting**

Contents

Getting Started

The projects in this book use lots of art **materials** that you will already have at home. Any missing materials can be found in an art supply store.

paintbrushes

clean water

For some of the projects, you will need to use a pair of scissors. Always ask an adult to help you.

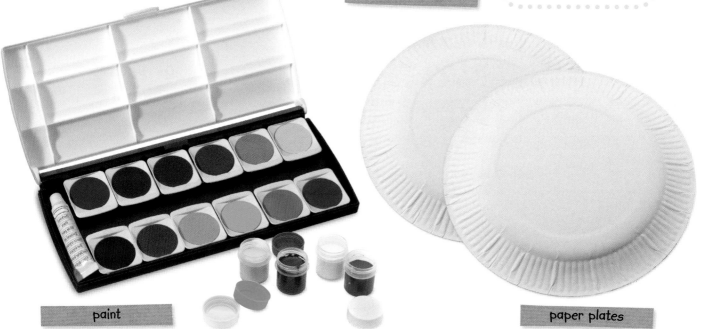

paint

paper plates

pebbles

pencil

sharpener

eraser

black felt-tip pen

Handy Hint

Acrylic paint has a glossy finish. When the paint is dry, it becomes water-resistant, which makes it perfect for many craft projects.

Here is a gallery of the paper you will need to complete all the painting projects.

Birds on a Wire

To make this picture of birds, you will need blue paper, a felt-tip pen, paints and paintbrushes.

1 Start this picture by drawing two thin lines across the paper. You can use a black felt-tip pen for this.

2 Now paint ovals onto the lines. These ovals will become the birds' bodies. Make them different colors.

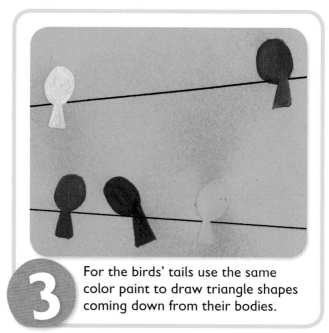

3 For the birds' tails use the same color paint to draw triangle shapes coming down from their bodies.

4 When the paint for the bodies has dried, use yellow paint to make small triangles for the birds' beaks.

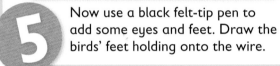

5 Now use a black felt-tip pen to add some eyes and feet. Draw the birds' feet holding onto the wire.

6 Finish your picture by painting the brown poles. Then add more birds!

Creepy House

To make this spooky picture, you will need black and white paint, brushes and orange paper.

1 Start this spooky picture by painting a large black area along the bottom of the paper. This will be the ground.

2 Use the black paint to form a shape on top of the ground. This will become the creepy house.

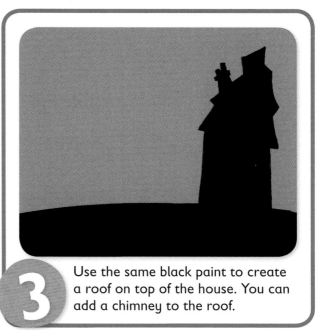

3 Use the same black paint to create a roof on top of the house. You can add a chimney to the roof.

4 Using the black paint, make the shape of a tree. Paint thin and pointy branches coming off the trunk.

5 Now use some white paint to add the moon. Also add some windows and a door to the house.

6 To finish this spooky picture, you could add some black bats flying in the sky.

Slippery Snake

This snake is easy to create.
You will need paper, paints,
brushes and a black felt-tip pen.

1 Start your snake picture by painting a bright green oval on some white paper. This will be the snake's head.

2 Now use the same green paint to add a long, wiggly body. Make sure that the end of the tail is pointed.

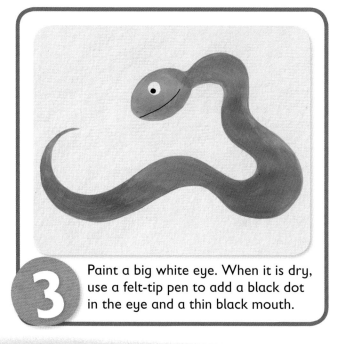

3 Paint a big white eye. When it is dry, use a felt-tip pen to add a black dot in the eye and a thin black mouth.

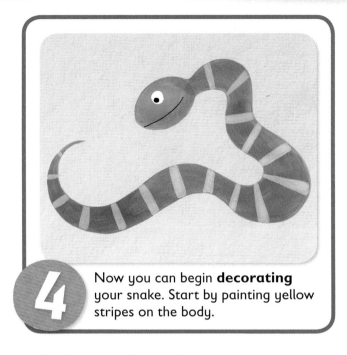

4 Now you can begin **decorating** your snake. Start by painting yellow stripes on the body.

5 Add blue triangles between the stripes. Remember to put a triangle on each side of the snake's body.

6 To finish the snake, add small red dots on the yellow stripes, and white dots in the blue triangles.

Garden Flowers

To make these pretty garden flowers, you will need some white paper, paints and paintbrushes.

1 Start your flower picture by painting a large yellow circle. This will become the center of the flower.

2 Now you can use some blue paint to add five large petals all the way around the center of the flower.

3 Use some green paint to make a stem. The stem should be a line that runs down from the flower.

4 Using the same green paint, you should now paint two large green leaves on either side of the stem.

5 You can add some green paint to the ground. This will make your flower look like it is growing in grass.

6 Put the finishing touches on this picture with bees, butterflies and more flowers.

14

Friendly Octopus

To make this friendly octopus, you will need paintbrushes, paints, a felt-tip pen and paper.

1 Start your underwater painting with a large purple circle. This circle will become the body of the octopus.

2 Paint some **tentacles** coming out of the octopus's body. Try to make them wavy.

3 When the purple paint has dried, use some blue paint to add suckers along the bottom of the tentacles.

4 Now take some white paint and make two large ovals on the body. These ovals will become the eyes.

5 Use a black felt-tip pen to add a big smile onto the octopus. Add some big black circles to his eyes.

6 Finish the picture by painting some seaweed and rocks. You could add some friendly fish, too.

Trees on a Hill

To make this picture of trees, you will need some white paper, some paints, brushes and a pencil.

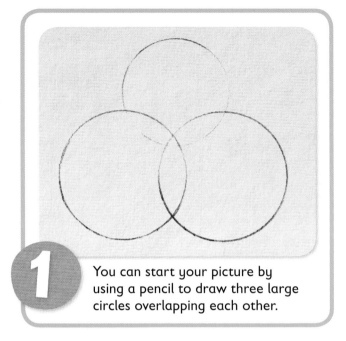

1 You can start your picture by using a pencil to draw three large circles overlapping each other.

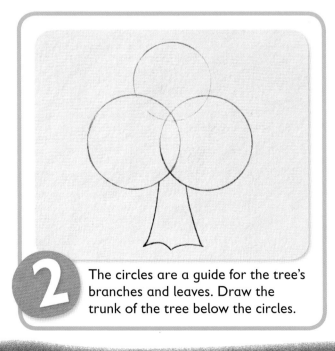

2 The circles are a guide for the tree's branches and leaves. Draw the trunk of the tree below the circles.

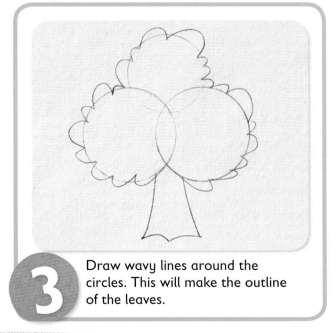

3 Draw wavy lines around the circles. This will make the outline of the leaves.

4 Use some of your brown paint to color the trunk of the tree. Try to follow the pencil lines carefully.

5 Now use some green paint to color the leaves of the tree. You can also add a blue cloud in the sky.

6 To finish this painting, add more trees in different shapes and sizes. Paint more clouds and some grass.

Stars in the Sky

To paint this exciting picture, you will need black paper, paints and some paintbrushes.

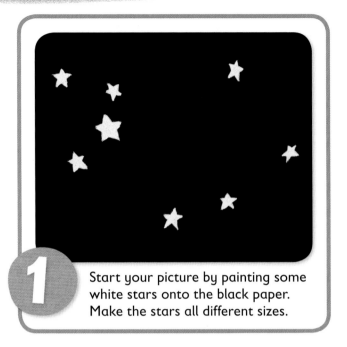

1 Start your picture by painting some white stars onto the black paper. Make the stars all different sizes.

2 Now you can add planets to your picture. Paint a ring around one of the **planets**.

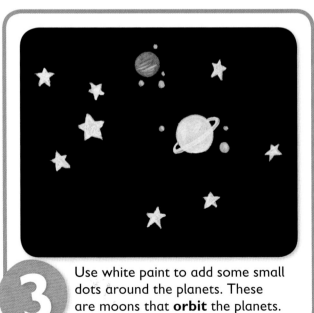

3 Use white paint to add some small dots around the planets. These are moons that **orbit** the planets.

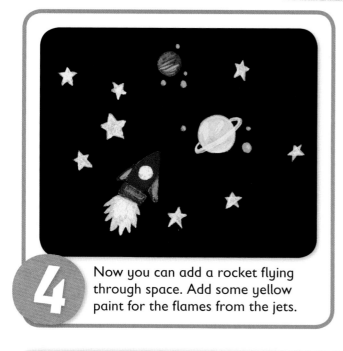

4 Now you can add a rocket flying through space. Add some yellow paint for the flames from the jets.

5 You can add a comet by painting a small yellow circle and then smudging it with a paintbrush.

6 Ask an adult to help you flick some white paint from a brush onto the paper to make tiny stars.

Pebble Bugs

To make these cute bugs, you will need some medium-sized pebbles, paints and paintbrushes.

1 Start by choosing a pebble that is a nice oval shape. Wash the stone and pat it dry with a clean paper towel.

2 Take some red paint and use it to paint the whole pebble. When you have finished, let it dry.

3 When the red paint is dry, use black paint to color the end of the stone. This will become the bug's face.

4 Paint a thin black line along the back of the bug to show the two wings. Now add black dots onto the wings.

5 Paint white circles for eyes onto the face, let them dry and then paint black dots on them.

6 You could try using different shaped stones and different colors to create a whole family of bugs.

Robot Masks

To make these fun masks, you will need paper plates, paints and some felt-tip pens.

1 Place a paper plate upside down on a table. Use some silver or grey paint to cover the whole plate.

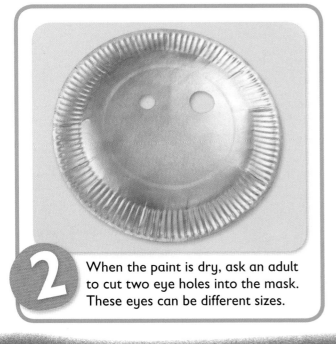

2 When the paint is dry, ask an adult to cut two eye holes into the mask. These eyes can be different sizes.

3 Now use some black paint to create a line of black circles across the front of the mask.

4 Use black paint to create a large semi-circle mouth. Don't forget to add some teeth to this mouth!

5 You can use more black paint to add a small rectangle in the middle of the plate for the nose of the robot.

6 Try making some more masks for your friends. You can use different colors and designs.

Glossary

word (pronunciation) definition

decorating (DEH-kuh-rayt-ing) Adding objects that make something prettier or more interesting.

materials (muh-TEER-ee-ulz) What things are made of.

orbit (OR-bit) To travel in a circular path. Bold on p. 18, box 3.

planets (PLA-nets) Large objects, such as Earth, that move around the Sun.

tentacles (TEN-tih-kulz) Long, thin growths on animals that are used to touch, hold, or move.

Index

Further Reading

Fisher, Diana. *Painting Techniques*. Irvine, CA: Walter Foster Publishing, 2004.

Wheeler, Annie. *Painting on a Canvas: Art Adventures for Kids*. Layton, UT: Gibbs Smith, 2006.

Websites

For web resources related to the subject of this book, go to:
www.windmillbooks.com/weblinks and select this book's title.